The World Famous

(WELL A FEW PEOPLE HAVE READ IT)

ABC

BOOK OF RHYMES

By
Roger Carlson

I0212392

A is for Apple, which grows on a tree.
Apples are yummy for people like me.

B is for Bouncing my big rubber ball.
If I bounce it hard, my ball bounces so tall..

C is for Camera, you point it and click. **C** It captures the moments that pass really quick.

D is for Doggie, curled up on my lap. When doggie's done playing, it's time for his nap.

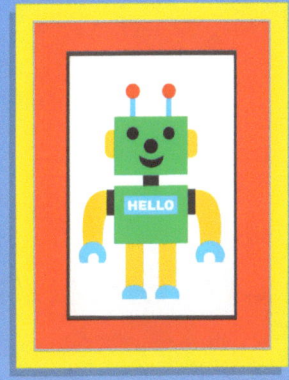

E is for Elephant; she sleeps standing up.
Her trunk is so long it can pick up my cup.

11

Fis for Farm, where the vegetables grow.
You're growing up too; didn't you know?

G is for Grandma, who grew up to be old. Grandmas have stories that love to be told.

His for Home; it can be big or quite small.
I hope yours is full of love from wall to wall.

I is for Igloo, made of ice blocks and snow.
Inuits lived in them a long time ago.

J is for Jungle, it's wild,
dense, and deep.
Pack your rain jackets and
climb in a jeep.

Kis for Kite; it flies high and swoops low.
It dances in the air as the winds blow.

L is for Lollipop, such a fun word to say.
It rolls off your tongue in the best kind of way.

M is for Moon, but it's not made of cheese. We can stay up to see it, if we say "pretty-please."

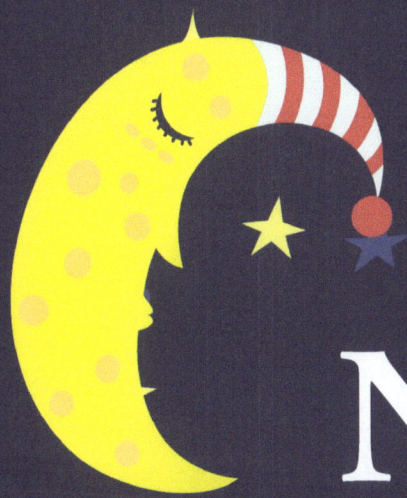

N is for Nest, where the little birds rest. Nighty-night little birds, sleep tight in the nest.

z-z-z

1

Ois for Owl, sitting high in a tree. Up on the tallest branch, where no one can see.

OVAL

P is for Popcorn that goes "Pop! Pop! Pop!"
Once you start eating, you really can't stop.

Q is for Quiet, when you're reading a book.
It's nice to be quiet and read in a nook.

R is for Rabbit; they jump fast and hop. It's hard to catch rabbits 'cause they just don't stop.

S is for Sunshine, which beams from up high. It warms the Earth from its place in the sky.

Tis for Turtle, he hides in **T**his shell.
When will it pop out? We really can't tell.

U is for Umbrella,
colorful and bright.
The rain comes down, and
you hold it upright.

V is for Vine,
growing grapes
that are sweet.
If you find a grapevine,
you're in for a treat.

Wis for World, or the place
we call home.
We need to respect it wherever we
roam.

X is the letter for "X marks the spot." What treasures you'll find if you find the X-dot.

Y is for Yawn, when a poem is too long.
I might fall asleep if you sing me a song.

YUMMY

YOGURT

Z is for Zero, the number for none.
After the zero, our poem is all done.

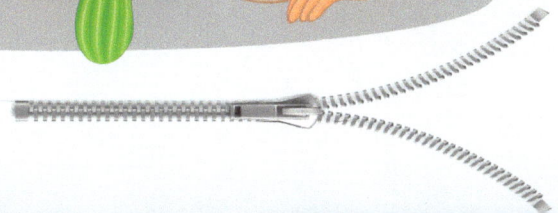

Practice saying words again here

Find these and all of the other Mariana Publishing books for sale on Amazon and our web site
www.marianapublishing.com

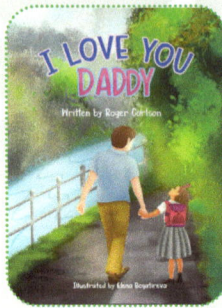

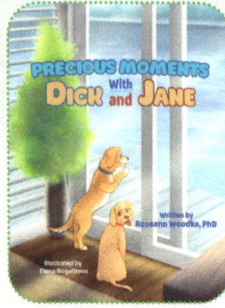

WAYBACK BOOKS

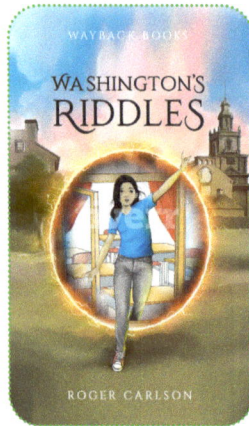

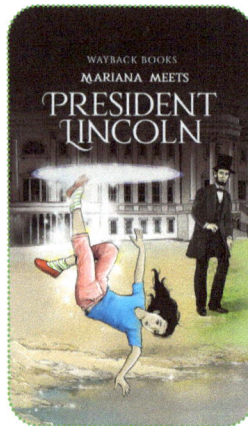

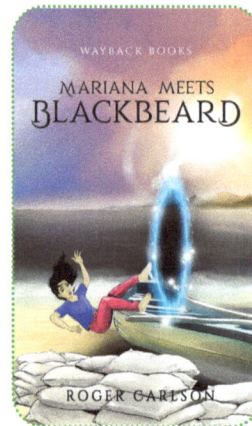

Find us on:

f @marianapublishing | @marianapublishing | @LlcMariana

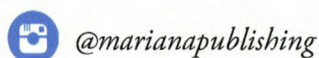

Copyright © 2020 by Roger Carlson
All rights reserved, including the right of reproduction in whole or in part in any form. This book or any portion thereof may not be reproduced or used in any manner whatsoever without the express written permission of the publisher except for the use of brief excerpts for review purposes.

ISBN: 978-1-64510-037-9 (Hardback)
ISBN: 978-1-64510-035-5 (Amazon Paperback)
ISBN: 978-1-64510-036-2 (Print On Demand)